In the Garden

Patricia Castle

I0807000

INFOMAX COMMON CORE READERS

Rosen Classroom™

New York

Published in 2013 by The Rosen Publishing Group, Inc.
29 East 21st Street, New York, NY 10010

Book Design: Michael J. Flynn

Photo Credits: Cover Margarita Borodina/Shutterstock.com; p. 4 Lucian Coman/Shutterstock.com; p. 5 Stefan Fierros/Shutterstock.com; p. 6 H. Brauer/Shutterstock.com; p. 7 Surkov Vladimir/Shutterstock.com; p. 8 Cousin_Avi/Shutterstock.com; p. 9 BESTWEB/Shutterstock.com; p. 10 Julija Sapic/Shutterstock.com; p. 11 Yuji Sakai/Digital Vision/Getty Images; p. 12 Igor Sokolov/Shutterstock.com; p. 13 Shutterstock.com; p. 14 Valentyn Volkov/Shutterstock.com; p. 15 Antonova Olena/Shutterstock.com.

ISBN: 978-1-4488-8944-0
6-pack ISBN: 978-1-4488-8945-7

Manufactured in the United States of America

CPSIA Compliance Information: Batch #WS12RC: For further information contact Rosen Publishing, New York, New York at 1-800-237-9932.

Word Count: 78

Contents

In the Garden 4

Plant Parts 15

Words to Know 16

Index 16

Jen likes working in her garden.

Jen plants seeds in the ground.

Jen sees green leaves in her garden.

Leaves take in light for her plants.

Jen sees stems in her garden.

Stems hold her plants up.

Jen sees roots in her garden.

Roots take in water for her plants.

Jen sees flowers in her garden.

The flowers are many colors.

Jen picks the flowers.

She puts them in a jug.

Jen picks fruits from her garden, too.

Plant Parts

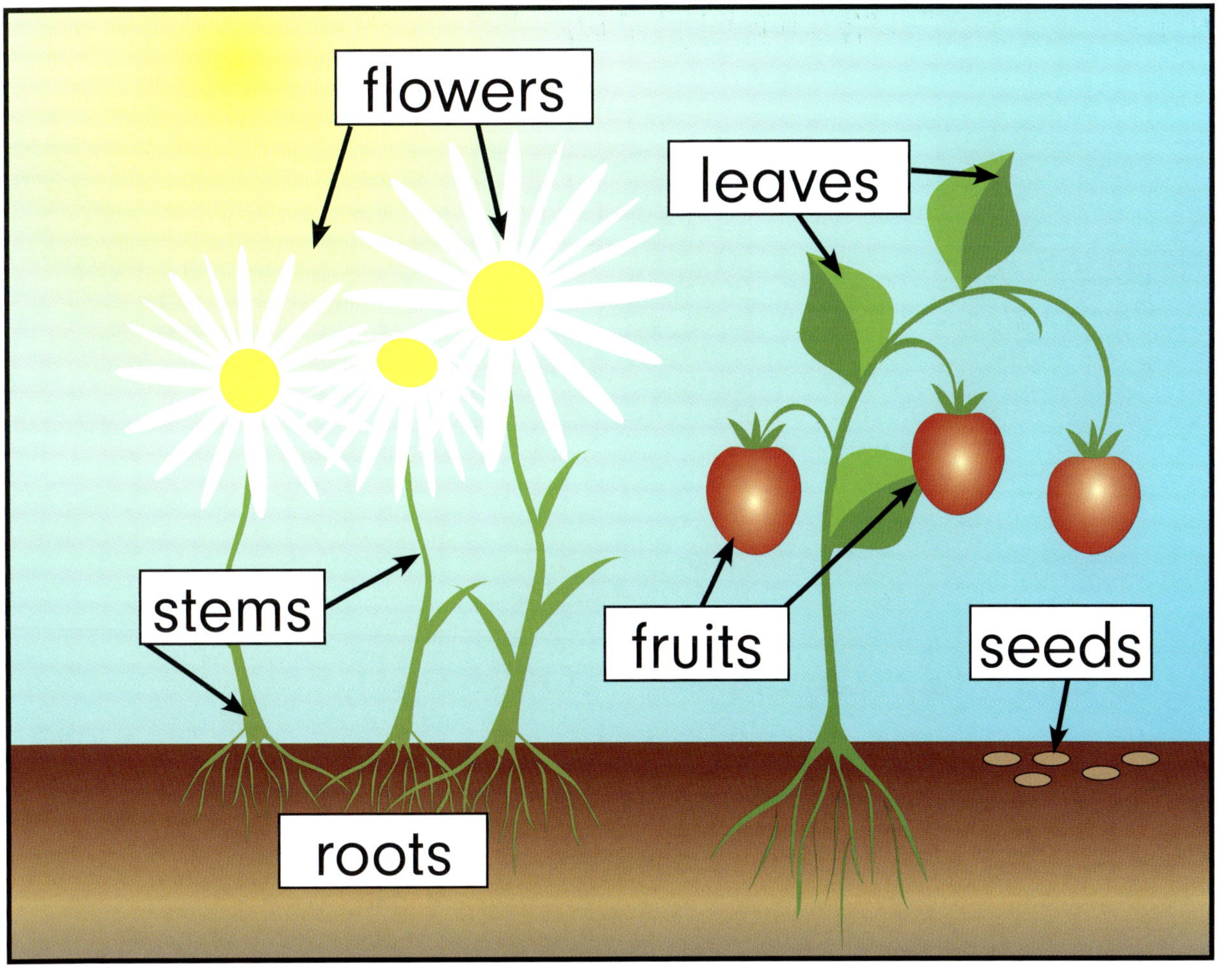

Words to Know

flowers

fruits

leaves

roots

seeds

stems

Index

flowers, 12, 13, 15

fruits, 14, 15

leaves, 6, 7, 15

roots, 10, 11, 15

seeds, 5, 15

stems, 8, 9, 15